Barn Owl Sees Town

Written by Charlotte Raby
Illustrated by Andy Rowland

Collins

barn owl up high

goat down in town

barn owl up high

goat down in town

barn owl in the park

near six ducks

barn owl in the park

near six ducks

barn owl hoots

coins on the soil

11

barn owl hoots

coins on the soil

15

🐾 Review: After reading 🐾

Use your assessment from hearing the children read to choose any GPCs, words or tricky words that need additional practice.

Read 1: Decoding
- Turn to pages 2 and 3. Draw the children's attention to the word **owl**. Can they find any other words with the GPC /ow/? (***down***, ***town***).
- Turn to pages 10 and 11. Ask the children to find and read the words with the sound /oi/. (***coins***, ***soil***).

Read 2: Vocabulary
- Go back through the book and discuss the pictures. Encourage the children to talk about details that stand out for them. Use a dialogic talk model to expand on their ideas and recast them in full sentences, as naturally as possible.
- Work together to expand vocabulary by naming objects in the pictures that children do not know.
- Ask the children to point to and read the word that answers these questions:
  - Page 8 – Where is the owl? (***park***)
  - Page 12 – What does the owl do? (***hoots***)

Read 3: Comprehension
- Have the children read or heard any other stories about owls? How were they like this one? How were they different?
- What time of day do you think it is in the story? What makes you think that?
- Turn to pages 14 and 15, and ask: What does the owl see in town?